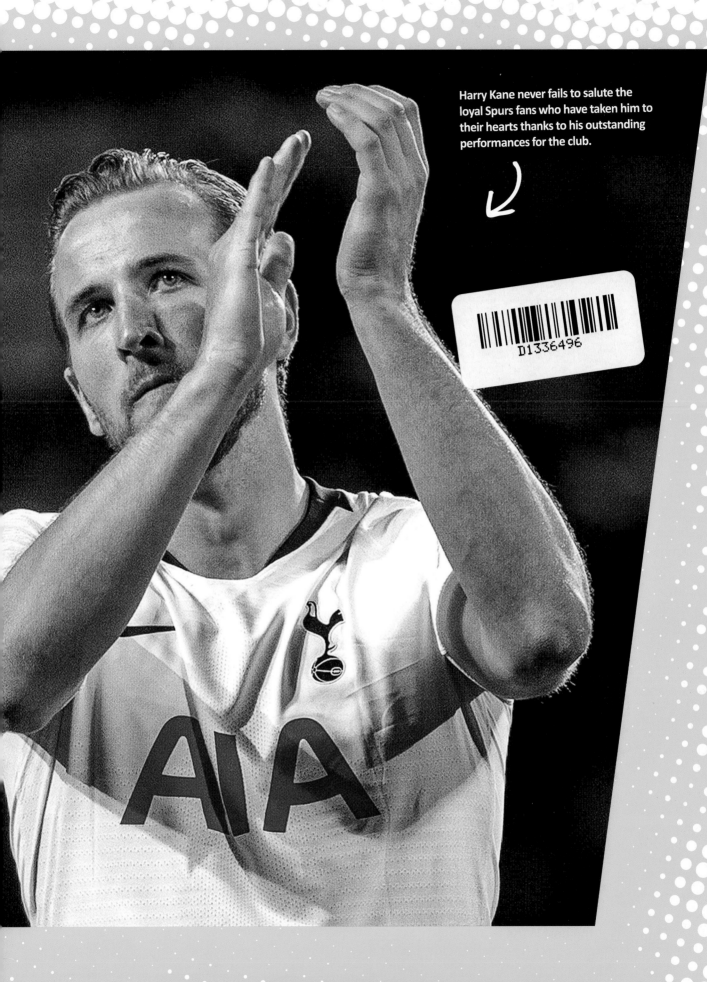

Harry Kane never fails to salute the loyal Spurs fans who have taken him to their hearts thanks to his outstanding performances for the club.

INTRODUCTION

"Harry Kane – he's one of our own!" rings out the chant of the Spurs faithful. Fans love nothing better than a local hero and they have celebrated every single goal Harry, who was born just a few miles away, has scored. He has helped take Tottenham Hotspur and England to heights they have not scaled for years and they have every reason to be incredibly proud of him.

In 2018, Harry captained England to the World Cup finals, where he led them to the semi-finals and won the Golden Boot as the tournament's leading scorer. It is a scenario that seemed impossible when Arsenal rejected him as a young boy and, as a teenager, Tottenham sent him out on a series of loans. But Harry's whole career has been driven by self-belief and a determination to succeed. He is acknowledged as one of the hardest-working players in the game – continually striving to improve his fitness and technique.

In 2014, Harry Kane announced himself as a Premier League striker, scoring 21 goals for Tottenham in just 34 games. Many dubbed him a one-season wonder, but Harry kept scoring, topping the Premier League goal-scoring charts in consecutive seasons. Meanwhile, those who doubted he could thrive on the international scene were silenced as he netted just 79 seconds into his England debut and continued to score with a strike-rate equalling that of some of the nation's greatest strikers.

Harry has proved he is the complete forward. He is equally comfortable with either foot or his head. He is deadly in the box, strikes incredible shots from distance, rarely misses a penalty, and increasingly makes chances for others with his vison and precise passing. He has scored against every Premier League club he has faced and is a proven big-match player, as shown by the incredibly cool penalties that helped England progress in the World Cup or his last-minute strike against Croatia in November 2018, which sent them to the UEFA Nations League semi-final.

In 2019, Harry Kane was awarded the MBE for his services to football. It was an honour he collected with pride, but those who have followed his career know that he will not rest there. He is determined to be the best in the world and take his club and country to the very top.

Captain and talisman for club and country: Harry Edward Kane.

THE YOUNG HARRY KANE

These days, football teams' big stars often come from far away – another country, or even a far-off continent. Tottenham Hotspur's biggest star, however, was born just a few miles from the ground.

Harry Kane grew up in Chingford, a London suburb a short journey from the sparkling new Tottenham Hotspur Stadium. Harry's parents were both born in Galway in Ireland, but had spent most of their lives in London. On 28 July 1993, they welcomed Harry Edward Kane into the world, a brother for their other young son Charlie. They were not a footballing family – although Harry has mentioned his maternal grandfather was a decent player – but the young lad showed some ability from an early age.

Joining local team Ridgeway Rovers' newly formed under-sevens team, Harry impressed immediately – as a goalkeeper! The coaches soon discovered he was even better outfield, banging in goals as a striker. "He could see a pass, he could play," remembers Ridgeway coach, Dave Bricknell. "He had good touch, but his main attribute was he had major confidence in himself."

With many Tottenham fans in his family, Harry also supported his local club. His favourite players were goalscoring legends Teddy Sheringham, himself a Chingford boy, and Jermain Defoe, who once parked his Range Rover to join Harry and his Year Seven mates playing street football. However, Harry's biggest hero was playing for Manchester United. David Beckham was also a local lad from north London. The England captain had played for Ridgeway Rovers, attended the secondary school that Harry would go to and had been picked up by Spurs Academy.

By the time he was eight, a Beckham-mohican-sporting Harry was following in his idol's footsteps – almost. However, it wasn't Tottenham scouts who spotted him, but those of rivals Arsenal. However, despite scoring freely for the young Gunners, Harry was released after a year. "He was a bit chubby and wasn't very athletic," said academy boss, Liam Brady. "We made a mistake."

Harry was gutted. "Since then, I've always had a chip on my shoulder," he later told the *Daily Mirror*. "I've always wanted to prove people wrong". In the *Players' Tribune* he wrote, "It might sound ridiculous – I was only eight when they let me go – but every time we played them, I thought, 'All right, we'll see who's right and who's wrong'."

Harry with his first ever football manager, Dave Bricknell, at a Ridgeway Rovers presentation in 2011.

A baby-faced Harry, and future wife Kate Goodland, meet his hero David Beckham, at the David Beckham Academy in 2005.

A Ridgeway Rovers training session with youngsters hoping to follow in the steps of former players David Beckham, Andros Townsend and Harry Kane.

ACADEMY DAYS

Harry returned to Ridgeway Rovers, but was too good not to get spotted again – this time by Watford. However, his time with the Hertfordshire club was also short: when Harry scored a hat-trick against them, Spurs decided to invite him to join their academy.

It was an offer Harry was never going to refuse. "The white kit fitted better on me," he said! He made steady progress in the Spurs Academy, but he wasn't turning heads. Not yet a teenager, he wasn't tall or quick. What did set Harry apart, though, were his attitude and determination. "He had a fantastic desire to improve and would always want to do extra work at the end of a session," recalled former Tottenham (now Liverpool) reserve coach, Alex Inglethorpe. "He became obsessive about his finishing in all its various forms and would dedicate a huge amount of time to improving these aspects of his game."

The practice paid off. Harry had grown physically and as a player and, in July 2009, on his 16th birthday, he signed an apprentice contract with Tottenham. The next season he scored 18 times in 22 games for the Under-18s, establishing himself as a dead-ball expert. He was now regularly training with the first team squad and in October 2009 he sat on the bench as an unused substitute, as Spurs took on Everton in the League Cup.

In February 2010, Harry received a call-up for the England Under-17s. As they trained for an international competition, the Algarve Cup in Portugal, England assistant coach Kenny Swain was impressed but, looking back, he admitted, "It wasn't so much his technical ability, but he had a thirst and an appetite for work, for goals, and wanting to learn and do better." Kane scored two goals in three matches at the tournament.

On his 17th birthday, Harry signed his first professional contract – he was on his way. However, opportunities for young players at the club were limited. Tottenham had recently withdrawn from the Premier Reserve League so, along with a number of other Spurs hopefuls, such as Danny Rose, Alex Pritchard, Andros Townsend, Tom Carroll and Ryan Mason, Harry would need a loan move to prove that he could make it in senior football.

With few opportunities for first team action, young Harry found himself among the subs.

A teenage Harry Kane in action for England Under-17s in 2010.

LOAN RANGER

League One football was pretty physical and no one was going to make an allowance for a teenager on loan from a big club, but Harry gritted his teeth and got on with the job.

In January 2011, Harry joined nearby Leyton Orient for the rest of the season, making nine starts and as many substitute appearances. He was still no sensation, but his finishing was admired – he scored on his first League start and racked up five goals in total.

Harry returned to Spurs the following season, with Tottenham manager Harry Redknapp keen to use his youngsters in their UEFA Europa League campaign. On 25 August 2011, Harry at last made his senior debut – against Edinburgh club Hearts. However, despite making six Europa League appearances and scoring his first Tottenham goal at Shamrock Rovers, Harry was soon off on loan again, joining League One club Millwall in the new year.

The Lions' fans were not too keen on players from their London rivals, but Harry soon won them round with his work rate and goals. With the club in relegation trouble, Harry's nine goals in 27 matches helped them to safety and saw him named as Millwall's Young Player of the Year. "I was 18, we were in a relegation battle and it turned me into a man," Harry later told the *Guardian*.

Harry was back at White Hart Lane for the 2012–13 season, impressing new boss André Villas-Boas with a hat-trick in a 6-0 pre-season thrashing of Southend United. It earned him a five-minute Premier League debut as a substitute in the first game of the season against Newcastle United.

By the end of August Harry was on loan again, though, this time at Premier League Norwich City. There, a broken bone in his foot limited him to just five goalless appearances. He was off to Leicester City for the second half of the season and, despite scoring on his home debut, once more he struggled to make an impact, famously sharing a subs' bench with Jamie Vardy.

In February 2013, Spurs offered Harry Kane a new four-year contract. They clearly believed in him, but as he returned to the club at the end of the season, assistant manager Tim Sherwood gave him an ultimatum: "No more loans – you get in the team or you get sold."

Harry spent the end of the 2010–11 season at Leyton Orient scoring five times in 18 appearances.

Harry found his feet at Millwall, winning their Young Player of the Year award in 2012.

EARNING HIS SPURS

It was a brave decision for Spurs boss Tim Sherwood to replace Roberto Soldado, Tottenham's record signing, with a 20-year-old who had experienced just a handful of first-team starts.

It was no hunch, though. Sherwood knew what Harry could offer, because he had been coaching him for four years and had guided him through his loan spells. "I looked at a kid on a training field against a £28m signing and I saw someone that was better than him," he said.

Sherwood took over from André Villas-Boas just before Christmas 2013. A. V .B. had relied on his big-name strikers – Emmanuel Adebayor, Jermain Defoe and Soldado – but between them they had delivered only 15 goals in 16 matches. Not that

Sherwood rushed to bring in his young protégé: it wasn't until April that he gave Harry the nod over Soldado, starting him against Sunderland.

In the 59th minute with the game locked at 1–1, Christian Eriksen curled a wicked low cross into the six-yard area and Spurs's number 37 was a foot ahead of the defenders, enough to tap it home. It was Harry's first Premier League strike. He went on to score a header against West Bromwich Albion in the next match, and another against Fulham made it three in consecutive games. There was no

The hat-trick hero takes over in goal against Asteras Tripoli.

Another goal in the locker for Harry. This one for Tottenham against Hull City in the League Cup at White Hart Lane in October 2013.

dropping him now and he kept his place for the final few games of the season.

By the start of the 2014–15 season, Tim Sherwood had been replaced by Mauricio Pochettino and Harry found himself back to square one. Pochettino had a reputation for developing young players, but also for being fair, and he was willing to offer another chance to Adebayor and Soldado ahead of Harry. The youngster's opportunities were limited to UEFA Europa League and Football League Cup matches, but he made the most of them, scoring in all but one of the early games.

On 23 October against Greek side Asteras Tripolis at White Hart Lane, Harry netted his first senior hat-trick and even took over in goal after Hugo Lloris was sent off. He only had a few minutes to keep a clean sheet, but conceded from the first shot he faced. The match confirmed two things: despite his self-belief, Harry would never make it as a goalkeeper, but as far as goalscoring was concerned, he was the real deal.

Harry sends a goalbound header in the UEFA Europa League round-of-16 tie against Benfica in 2014.

ONE-SEASON WONDER

Mauricio Pochettino couldn't ignore the claims of his young striker forever and, given the chance, the 21-year old made sure the manager would never regret his decision...

By November 2014, with his strikers misfiring and substitute Harry's deflected free-kick having given Spurs a last-minute victory at Aston Villa, Pochettino finally gave Harry a Premier League start. Despite a series of indifferent results, the now number 18 continued to score and make chances, and deservedly kept his place in the team.

Those who had not yet heard of Spurs's new star were about to discover just what he could do. On 1 January 2015 League leaders Chelsea came to White Hart Lane and received a Kane-inspired 5–3 thrashing. Harry scored two and won a penalty and the *Daily Telegraph* lavished praise, writing "Kane was unplayable at times, too strong, too determined and the model of composure when enduring some rough challenges."

Another brace followed soon, against West Brom, but the North London derby against Arsenal in February was the match that fans anticipated most and Harry didn't disappoint. A far-post prod home from a flicked-on corner and a wonderful glancing header sank the Gunners. "It's my first North London derby after watching so many as a kid," he told *BBC Sport*. "It's magical. It's a feeling I can't describe and won't forget."

Kane was now regularly making the headlines. He was named Premier League Player of the Month in January and February; celebrated his full England call-up with a first Premier League hat-trick against Leicester City; captained Tottenham for the first time in a 0–0 draw at Burnley; and became the first Spurs player to score 30 goals in a season since Gary Lineker in 1991–92. His 21-goal tally was bettered only by Sergio Aguero, and he was voted PFA Young Player of the Year. Not bad for a player whose first League start had come in November.

Harry's goals had helped Spurs to a UEFA Europa League spot and to the Football League Cup final – a defeat against Chelsea the big disappointment in his great season. He said it felt like he had almost squeezed a whole career into just one campaign. Spurs fans had a new hero, but many other teams' supporters were still not convinced: "He's just a one-season wonder," they claimed.

Harry poses with his PFA Young Player of the Year trophy in 2015.

Harry strikes against Newcastle United in December 2014 – defenders were now getting to know and fear Spurs' new striker.

In action against Chelsea in the 2015 League Cup final.

ONE OF OUR OWN

For the 2015–16 season Harry, now the only senior striker at the club, took the number ten shirt once worn by his heroes Teddy Sheringham and Robbie Keane. In doing so, he carefully explained that he changed his number "to become a club legend."

The season didn't start well. After ten league games Harry had scored as many in his own net as the opponents' – one. The "One-season Wonder" brigade were out in force. A hat-trick at Bournemouth in October and nine more by the end of the year, including his first at the Emirates and two against West Ham, silenced the doubters.

In the New Year, Harry spearheaded Spurs' best run at a league title for 55 years. Wearing a mask to protect his nose broken in an FA Cup tie against Crystal Palace, he averaged a goal a game in a 14-match unbeaten run. Spurs finally gave up the chase on unstoppable Leicester City with two games left, but they had given everything. Harry's consolation was his tally of 25 league goals in the season, which landed him his first Golden Boot. He was the first Englishman to win it in 16 years.

The 2016–17 season was Tottenham's last at their iconic White Hart Lane stadium before it was demolished to make way for the new stadium. Despite again failing to score in August, Harry resumed his fantastic strike rate, until two lengthy ankle injuries sidelined him. His goals – including hat-tricks against Stoke City and West Bromwich Albion – drove Spurs towards another title challenge, but they could only finish runners-up behind Chelsea.

Harry had hit a hat-trick at Fulham in an FA Cup run that took them to a semi-final against Chelsea. His instinctive stooping header levelled the scores but, despite looking stronger, Tottenham were once again thwarted by the west Londoners.

Another "nearly" season was sweetened for Harry when he scored in a 2–1 victory over Manchester United – Tottenham's final goal in their farewell game at White Hart Lane. Then incredibly, in the final two games of the season, he won the Golden Boot again, as four goals in a 6–1 demolition of Leicester City and three in a 7–1 thrashing of Hull City took his season tally to an unmatched 29.

Spurs fans lamented the near misses, but now they knew they had an exceptional young team with a world-class player in their ranks – and he was one of their own.

Now a marked man, Harry takes on Borussia Dortmund's German international Mats Hummels.

At just 22 years of age, Harry was already a hero at White Hart Lane.

ENGLAND EXPECTS

Harry first pulled on the England shirt as a teenager and it was a significant moment – "Playing for your country is a magical moment and for me it was the start of everything I dreamed of achieving as a senior player."

In 2010, 16-year-old Harry was called up to the Under-17s squad for the Algarve International tournament. Within a year he was turning out for the Under-19s, scoring twice on his debut against Albania and starring in their UEFA European Championship campaign, despite often playing in midfield. His goal against France took England to the semi-finals, but he was rested as the team succumbed to Greece.

Harry scored six goals in 14 games for the England Under-19 team.

Harry celebrates after helping England to a famous 3–2 victory over Germany in Berlin in March 2016.

By the time Euro 2016 arrived, Harry had established himself as England's major attacking threat.

Harry then stepped up to the Under-21s, making his debut for manager Gareth Southgate against Scotland in August 2013. He hit a hat-trick against San Marino in his second match and was integral to the team's progress to the 2015 UEFA European Championships, scoring six times in the qualifiers. By now, Harry had already won his first full England cap. After his 2014–15 goalscoring feats, manager Roy Hodgson selected him for the Euro qualifiers in March 2015.

Harry didn't disappoint. Replacing Wayne Rooney after 71 minutes against Lithuania, it took him just 79 seconds to get on the scoresheet, creating space to nod home at the far post with just his third touch. "Hurry Kane", "Prince Harry" and "Kane You Believe It?" read the excited back-page headlines.

Martin O'Neill claimed that back in 2014 Kane's agent had suggested he might choose to play for Ireland, but Harry's only ambition was to represent England. Four days after the Lithuania match, he made his full England debut against Italy. This time he didn't score and he would experience more disappointment when he returned to the Under-21s for an uninspiring team display in the Euros.

Harry was now battling for a place in the senior team, and his vital goals as a substitute gave Hodgson little choice but to start him. When Harry's low finish sparked a sensational 3–2 friendly victory over Germany in March, hopes were high for the Euros in France. However, England and their new marksman failed to spark – Hodgson was criticized for sending Kane to take corners, while others claimed Harry was exhausted or even not up to the challenge of high-profile tournaments. Once again, he was determined to prove the doubters wrong.

HARRY AT HOME

On the pitch and in training Harry is a football obsessive, but off-duty he's a dedicated family man who loves his golf and American Football.

Harry is the complete family man. He still lives near his parents on the borders of Essex and north London, is close to his brother Charlie and is devoted to his wife Katie Goodland and young daughters Ivy and Vivienne Jane. They all know him as "H" – a name his friends and family have used since his schooldays.

It was at secondary school that Harry and Katie first met. The press have unearthed a photograph taken in 2005 when, aged 11 and 12 respectively, they were pictured with David Beckham at the launch of his football academy. Despite once sharing a teenage kiss, they only began dating in 2012 and became engaged in 2017 after Harry proposed on a beach in the Bahamas. They seem so suited, especially as Katie is a sports science graduate and works as a fitness instructor!

Mauricio Pochettino has disclosed that Harry is so completely focused on his football that he spends the week at a house he owns close to the training ground. His family home, however, has graced the pages of celebrity magazines and reveals how he spends his free time. Photos show him playing with his daughters, but also his "man den" where he plays video games, the state-of-the-art gym with walls adorned in his framed Spurs and England shirts, and a home cinema room which also contains a golf simulator.

Harry is, of course, a keen and talented golfer. He has a handicap of four and in November 2018 shot an under-par round at a Hertfordshire course that hosted the British Masters. He is also an American Football obsessive. He is a fan of the New England Patriots, his two Labrador dogs are named after gridiron stars Tom Brady and Russell Wilson, and he admitted that he has ambitions of being an NFL kicker once his soccer playing days have finished.

Harry doesn't drink alcohol and shies away from London's trendy clubs, preferring the company of family and close friends. He enjoys hosting a barbeque, even if he occasionally over-indulges on steak – and chastises himself afterwards for his weakness. That's Harry – a completely grounded guy, totally dedicated to his family and to improving as a footballer.

A proud Kane family attend Buckingham Palace as Harry receives his MBE.

Ivy Kane joins her daddy on the pitch at Wembley.

23

SUPER STRIKER

Harry won the Premier League Golden Boot twice by the age of 23 and in January 2019 became the first player to score against every Premier League side he has faced. But just what makes him so deadly in front of goal?

HEADING

Around one in seven of Harry's goals are from headers. Tall and strong, he is naturally good in the air, but scoring with the head requires a deft touch and a heightened awareness of position. He is exceptional at peeling off defenders at the back post, at powerful or glancing headers from deep crosses (a classic came in the North London derby at Wembley in February 2018) or by just getting ahead of defenders, as in his stooping header in the FA Cup semi-final against Chelsea in April 2017.

Hot-shot Harry – deadly from three or 30 yards.

PENALTIES

As a youngster Harry had a reputation as a pretty lethal dead-ball merchant. Now he often leaves that role to Spurs team-mates Christian Eriksen or Kieran Trippier, while his penalty-taking remains impossible to predict. The 2018 FIFA World Cup displayed his ability to perform under pressure. He blasted one penalty into the top corner, chipped one down the middle and, taking England's first in the shoot-out against Colombia, fired a low shot into the side-netting.

SHOOTING

Harry loves to take a shot. He is happy to strike with either foot and his opportunism often takes keepers by surprise. Equally, his power and accuracy can leave them standing. He is especially adept at cutting in from the wing and curling a shot from distance (the strike against Arsenal at White Hart Lane in March 2016 was one to savour), or hitting pin-point accurate low shots into the corner.

Harry has become the penalty king, for club and country.

POACHING

"He only scores tap-ins" say Harry's detractors. But if it's so easy, why isn't everyone doing it? Harry is an expert at anticipating the chance, being aware of space and having the strength to muscle himself into position. And when the opportunity arrives, he has the composure – taking an extra touch when he can – and technique to find the back of the net.

The man just loves scoring goals!

HARRY'S GREAT SPURS GOALS (1)

Harry is a goal machine – scoring with his right foot, left foot or with his head. He's always in the right place for a tap-in, has a cool head for a penalty, but he's also collected a fair few unforgettable strikes.

TOTTENHAM HOTSPUR VS ARSENAL
Premier League
5 March 2016

A goal against the bitter rivals is always one to savour – and Harry has scored more Premier League goals against Arsenal than any other Spurs player. This one was particularly special. A clever back-heel from Dele Alli by the corner flag put Harry in space and he reached the penalty area just ten yards from the line. It was an impossible angle for a shot, but he still sent in a wicked curling strike that sailed over the defenders, past David Ospina's desperate dive and crashed into the net.

TOTTENHAM HOTSPUR VS CHELSEA
Premier League
1 January 2015

If football fans hadn't heard of Harry Kane before, they had now. Harry inspired Spurs' 5–3 demolition of the league leaders, with his first goal the pick of the lot. On the half-hour, Danny Rose fed the striker the ball on the left and Harry took off. Cutting inside, he evaded Branislav Ivanovic, went past Oscar, Cesc Fabregas and then Oscar again until he reached the centre of the pitch, where he unleashed a low 25-yard drive into the corner of the net.

TOTTENHAM HOTSPUR VS BORUSSIA DORTMUND
UEFA Champions League
13 September 2017

This was twenty seconds that showed what Harry is capable of. Strength: he was by the touchline on the halfway line when a lofted clearance came his way so he turned while wrestling a defender to the ground. Determination: he bulldozed another out of the way. Pace: Harry accelerated towards goal, passing another defender with a burst of speed. Finishing: with precision and power he beat the keeper with an emphatic near-post finish.

Taking on and beating Juventus and Italy's goalkeeping great Gigi Buffon.

JUVENTUS VS TOTTENHAM HOTSPUR
UEFA Champions League
13 February 2018

With Spurs trailing 2–0 away from home, they needed something special to get back into the game. It came in the 35th minute when Dele Alli spotted Harry's clever run across the defensive line and slotted a fine weighted pass through. Harry still had the great Gigi Buffon to beat in a one-on-one, but he did it with composure and style, taking the ball wide and keeping his balance to judge the angled shot perfectly.

Putting the finish on a perfect solo goal against Borussia Dortmund.

HE'S GOT IT ALL

There's more to Harry than goals. His skills have improved so rapidly that he is now a magnificent all-round player and an inspirational leader to boot.

If Harry's first seasons were spent proving he was the deadliest of strikers, his last few have shown that his all-round ability matches his finishing. Harry has adapted his game; dropping deep as a playmaker, using his strength and becoming a leader on and off the field. He is the complete footballer.

PASSING

Breaking down disciplined defences requires movement and creativity. Harry's ability to drop deep and become a playmaker has been a key addition to his skill set. His long-range passing, where he switches play from one side of the pitch to the other, is now a regular feature of his game. A great example is his superb assist for Son Heung-min against Huddersfield Town at Wembley in March 2018, when he held off a defender and sent a raking cross-field ball into his team-mate's path.

HOLD-UP PLAY

No sharp-shooting predator likes to be on the halfway line with his back to goal, but in the modern game it's a necessity. When Spurs or England are under pressure, Harry makes himself available. He has worked hard to improve his upper-body strength and his hold-up play has benefited, whether shielding the ball to allow midfielders to support him or turning to create opportunities – as in his brilliant spin-and-pass assist for Marcus Rashford for England against Spain in the Nations League.

Strong and determined, Harry can hold the ball even against the toughest defenders.

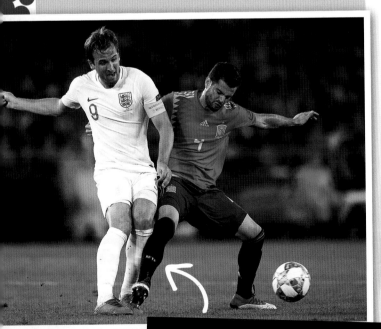

Harry's fabulous passing helped undo Spain in England's superb 2018 victory.

RUNNING WITH THE BALL

Harry in full flow is a sight to behold – and a pretty scary one for defenders! He has strength, balance, control and is comfortable with both feet. Even from the tightest of situations he invariably emerges with the ball and if space opens up (think Chelsea in 2015 or Borussia Dortmund in 2017), he needs no second invitation to shoot.

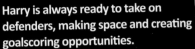

Harry is always ready to take on defenders, making space and creating goalscoring opportunities.

LEADERSHIP

Harry was just 21 years-old when he captained Spurs for the first time and though he has mostly been a deputy to Hugo Lloris, there is no doubting his influence in the dressing room. Even when injured, his half-time talk was said to have inspired the amazing Champions League comeback against Ajax. His leadership qualities were recognized by Gareth Southgate when he made him captain for the World Cup finals in Russia. Harry responded by leading from the front. Always positive, he drove the team on and remained professional on and off the pitch.

Harry's influence as a leader on the pitch for Spurs and England continues to grow.

CAPTAIN OF ENGLAND

In his first 17 appearances for England, Harry scored five goals. It was a reasonable strike rate, but it failed to match his astonishing tally for Tottenham. Could he up his game on the international stage?

As new manager Sam Allardyce took over, Harry played in a 1–0 win in Slovakia. However, he was once again starved of support and decent supply, and there were no immediate signs that England and Harry Kane were going to bounce back after the disappointment of Euro 2016.

Allardyce's sudden departure, however, saw Gareth Southgate take over as England boss. Unfortunately, an ankle injury initially kept Harry out of the team, but Southgate had been his coach in the England Under-21s and believed he could get the best out of the striker. By the time

Harry quickly developed a great relationship with England boss Gareth Southgate.

He leads his country with immense honour and great dignity.

England faced Scotland in a crucial FIFA World Cup qualifier in June 2017, Harry was fit and in possession of the Premier League Golden Boot. Southgate showed his confidence in the striker – not only picking him, but also naming Harry as his captain.

Captain Kane justified the coach's faith. He became England's hero when, four minutes into added time, he ghosted in at the far post to volley home Sterling's cross for a last-gasp equalizer. The floodgates were open. Three days later Harry struck twice in a 2–3 defeat in a friendly against France and, in the autumn, hit four in four World Cup qualifiers, including another injury-time strike against Slovenia which secured England's place at the finals.

In January, members of the England Supporters Club voted Harry their Player of the Year, with the Spurs star receiving 75 per cent of the vote. Despite Eric Dier and Jordan Henderson having worn the captain's armband in recent internationals, Southgate again named Kane as England's skipper for the finals – at 24-years old. He would be the nation's youngest ever major tournament captain, leading the youngest and least experienced squad in Russia.

England fans, bruised by recent tournament performances, had understandably modest hopes for the team, but Captain Kane declared himself optimistic: "I can't say we're not going to win it, because we could. I want to win everything I do, it's my mind-set, and so do the players. We're going to fight and give everything we've got."

On the field the England skipper is an inspirational figure.

HARRY IN NUMBERS

141 The number of games it took Harry to reach 100 Premier League goals – the second-fastest after Alan Shearer.

28 Harry has scored against 28 different teams in the Premier League – every single one he has ever faced.

13 The number of goals he has scored against his former loan club Leicester City in 12 appearances (only eight of those were starts).

10 Harry's current squad number for Spurs. He has previously worn 37 (2009–14) and 18 (2014–15).

56

The number of goals (including eight hat-tricks) Harry scored in 2017– the most by any player in Europe.

24

Harry netted his 24th European goal against Borussia Dortmund in 2019, overtaking Jermain Defoe to set new club record.

20

He has scored 22 England goals in 39 appearances at an average of 0.56 goals per game. At that rate, he will break Rooney's record of 53 England goals in his 96th appearance.

The numbers suggest Harry could eventually overtake Wayne Rooney as England's all-time top goalscorer.

200 million

In January 2019, the CIES Football Observatory valued Harry Kane at €200.3million (approximately £180million).

0.7

The average number of goals Harry scored in each league game as at the end of January 2019. It is the best strike-rate in Premier League history.

HARRY'S HAPPY TEAM-MATES

Even the greatest strikers need players around them to create chances. Fortunately, Harry has some of the best in the business to help him, and like all great strikers, he often repays the favour as well.

Harry has played with many greats. As a youngster he trained with Luka Modric, made his debut as Gareth Bale's team-mate and lined up alongside Wayne Rooney for England. As Harry has blossomed into a world-class player in his own right, he has developed a special relationship with certain team-mates.

The Korean superstar Son Heung-min and Harry present a deadly double threat.

Christian Eriksen

The Danish playmaker is the man who makes Tottenham tick. He is an assist-machine – featuring in the Premier League's top five goal-makers in every season since 2015–16 – and consistently puts the ball on a plate for his strikers. That's a godsend for Harry, whether Eriksen sends him off with a long defence-splitting ball, finds a deadly pass through a bank of defenders, or fizzes a cross into a space that's just perfect for a Kane glancing header.

The great Dane, Christian Eriksen, provider of so many of Harry's goals celebrates one of his own.

Son Heung-min

Their celebratory handshake might be a little cringeworthy, but Harry and Sonny's on-field combination is often devastating. Son likes to make direct runs and play upfront, allowing Harry to drop deeper and make things happen. With Sonny's runs behind the defence, he is often the recipient of Harry's passes and when that results in a stunning strike and a goal, who would deny them their friendship handshake?

The Dele and Harry show comes good again!

Raheem Sterling

Harry is often described as a great but humble player who just wants to work hard and get better, but those are also qualities Harry recognizes in his England team-mate. The Manchester City star's emergence in the national team has brought pace, trickery and assists to the front line, and Sterling has also taken some of the goal-scoring burden from the Spurs striker's shoulders.

Dele Alli

The Dele–Kane link-up has become a key element of Spurs' and England's play. Since Dele arrived from MK Dons in 2015, the pair have developed an almost telepathic on-field relationship. Harry has benefited from so many runs, flicks and passes from his team-mate, and he credits Dele with the ability to "change a game in a second". Meanwhile, Dele modestly admits, "Fitting in behind someone like Harry, you don't have to do too much."

THE HURRIKANE

As Harry kept on scoring throughout the 2017–18 season, records continued to tumble – at Tottenham, in the league and even across Europe.

Things were tough for Tottenham as the 2017–18 season got underway. They were playing home games at Wembley, did not win any of the first three games there and, once again, despite firing 25 shots, Harry had had a barren August.

If others were nervous, Harry wasn't. He scored with his first attempt in September – a fluke cross from the touchline against Everton. It was his 100th goal for Spurs in just 169 games. A brace in that match was followed with another double against West Ham and, breaking the so-called "Wembley jinx", yet another against Huddersfield.

Now barely a game passed without Kane getting on the scoresheet. Memorable moments included running Liverpool's defence ragged, the coolest side-foot finish against Stoke City and successive hat-tricks against Burnley and Southampton. The latter was his sixth league hat-trick in 2017 – just one of the new records he set.

His first against the Saints took Harry past Alan Shearer's record for the most Premier League goals scored in a calendar year (doing it in six fewer games) and his 2017 tally – for both club and country – was 56, passing Barcelona's Lionel Messi to become that year's supreme scorer across Europe. When Harry soared high to nod in yet another goal to beat Arsenal in February, *Match of the Day* pundit Danny Murphy summed it up: "Kane is fantastic, a big-game player. His all-round game is phenomenal."

When an ankle injury sustained at Bournemouth threatened to ruin his season, Harry proved a remarkably fast healer too, missing just one match. However, the season would again end in disappointment as Spurs were knocked out of the UEFA Champions League by Juventus and, in the FA Cup, where Harry had been instrumental in a run to the semi-final, they went down 2–1 in an agonizing match against Manchester United.

Harry was named in the PFA Team of the Year for the fourth consecutive season, but missed out on a third successive Golden Boot by two goals to Liverpool's Mo Salah. Tottenham finished third (pretty good for a team without a home!) and Harry signed a new contract to keep him at the club until 2024.

Harry shows off the match ball, having hit the perfect hat trick – left foot, right foot, header – against Apoel Nicosia in the Champions League.

2017 was an astonishing year for Harry as he racked up 56 goals across all competitions.

2018 FIFA WORLD CUP

Against all expectations, Harry led England's young lions to a FIFA World Cup semi-final and collected the prized Golden Boot.

Harry went to Russia hoping to put the disappointments of his last two international tournaments – the Under-21s UEFA European Championships and the 2016 Euros – behind him. He was captaining an England team whose refreshing approach had won over a cynical public who nevertheless had modest expectations for the young squad.

As England progressed through the group stage, the world took notice. Here was an exciting team who were dangerous at set pieces and had a world-class predator in their captain, Harry Kane. After just 11 minutes of their first group match against Tunisia, he calmly tapped home to send England on their way and, in added-time, won the game with a twisting far post header. Against

The right man at the right time. Harry gets England's World Cup campaign running with a late, late winner against Tunisia in Volgograd.

rough-tackling Panama, he hammered home two first-half penalties and completed a World Cup hat-trick in the second half with one of the luckiest goals of his career – a Loftus-Cheek long-range shot that deflected off Harry's heel.

Harry was rested for the final group game, but was reinstated for the round of 16 match against Colombia. Once again Harry executed a perfect penalty – this time straight down the middle. When the match ended even, Harry led from the front, stepping up to take England's opener in their first shootout win for 22 years, this time hitting it low past the keeper's right hand.

Harry had now scored in all eight of his games as England captain and been named official Man of the Match in every game he had played in the finals. Both came to an end in the quarter-finals, but he still led England to a 2–0 victory over Sweden. However, Harry's luck finally ran out in the semi-finals against Croatia. With England leading 1–0, a Kane shot rebounded to the striker and seemed a certain goal, but miraculously the keeper got the slightest touch to deflect it onto the post. Croatia rallied and in extra time scored to eliminate England at the final hurdle.

The whole team were devastated, even though they had exceeded expectations and given fans at home a reason to feel proud. For Harry, there was one consolation. His six goals were the most scored by any player in the finals and he became only the second Englishman ever to be awarded the Golden Boot.

Gareth Southgate presents Harry with his World Cup Golden Boot ahead of England's match against Spain in September 2018.

LET'S TALK ABOUT HARRY

"He scores poacher's goals, great goals, takes free kicks, takes penalties. He does the whole thing."
Gary Lineker

"Harry Kane is the best player in the world in terms of mental strength, willpower and endeavour."
Mauricio Pochettino

"I find it hard to find the words to describe him. I am in love like the fans are in love, like his team-mates are in love."
Mauricio Pochettino

40

"Kane is a dream of a player, dream of a professional."
Gary Neville

Alan Shearer believes Harry could eventually beat his record of 260 Premier League goals.

"Harry is the best goal-scorer in the world."
Gareth Southgate

"He is very good at everything. But what he does, he always does it towards the goal. He does not just stay [still] on the field, but he always attacks space at speed. He is a complete player. He did not seem to be one, but in the end, he is!"
Zinedine Zidane

"The 'HurriKANE' is part tempest, part deadly breeze."
Paul Hayward, *Daily Telegraph*

"He never gets stick from me when he's 'selfish' in a Spurs shirt – strikers score goals by shooting! But the way in which he is dropping off and bringing other players into the game is another sign of a brilliant and intelligent footballer."
Alan Shearer

AMONG THE WORLD'S BEST

Just 27 days after England's World Cup semi-final, Harry Kane was back in a Spurs shirt for the opening Premier League game of the 2018–19. Now rated as one of the world's great strikers could he inspire Tottenham to even greater heights?

It didn't take long for Harry to prove one point: he could score in August. In Tottenham's second game, a classic Kane check inside and cool shot against Fulham saw to that. To prove it was no fluke, he got another goal in the following match, a towering header to begin a 3–0 thrashing of Manchester United at Old Trafford.

As usual Harry took his place among the league's leading scorers; a 25-yard strike against Chelsea, an emphatic penalty against Arsenal and a rebound off his knee against Cardiff to complete his set of scoring against every Premier League team, among the highlights. As he led England to the Nations League semi-finals and powered Spurs' Champions League progress, Harry was named in the top ten of the Ballon D'Or for a second consecutive year.

The goals kept coming – poacher's goals, penalties and a 25-yard left-foot screamer

A memorable strike against Dortmund showcased Harry's talents to the whole of Europe.

against Wolves – while Spurs fans noticed how he was increasingly acting as a playmaker, with a magnificent assist for Dele Alli in a 2–0 Carabao (League) Cup win at the Emirates serving as a perfect example. The Carabao Cup looked like a good opportunity for Harry to pick up his first medal when he assuredly converted a penalty in the first leg of the semi-final against Chelsea, but by time the tie was completed Harry was injured. Missing Dele and Son too, Spurs took the tie to penalties but failed to make the final.

Harry came back from injury with a flurry of goals including another penalty against Arsenal which increased his position as the leading scorer in Premier League matches between the rivals. In the opening game at Spurs' new stadium against Crystal Palace, Harry was hoping to baptize it with a goal. Brought down with a jinking run, he might have earned a penalty, but Christian Eriksen was on hand to finish the move. His injury in the next home game, the Champions League quarter-final against Manchester City, brought his season crashing down and that new stadium goal would have to wait.

Despite the injuries, Harry still finished the season with 24 goals and was Tottenham's top scorer for the fifth successive season – a feat last achieved 45 years earlier by Martin Chivers. Still only 26, Harry is yet to reach his peak as a player. Already ranked among the world's best, who knows what he can achieve in the coming seasons.

Harry still loves tormenting North London rivals Arsenal.

HARRY'S GREAT SPURS GOALS (2)

These days, defenders know what Harry Kane is capable of. They mark him tightly or double up on him, but he keeps on scoring – even when it requires breathtaking skill, incredible composure or pin-point accuracy.

TOTTENHAM HOTSPUR VS BARCELONA
UEFA Champions League
3 October 2018

For once, Lionel Messi was admiring someone else's world-class skills. Harry had little on when he received the ball outside the area. From a standing start he took on defender Nélson Semedo on the outside, prompting the full-back to slide to block Harry's left-footed shot. Instead, Harry pulled the ball back and took half a second to assess the situation before curling a right-footed shot around the oncoming Gerard Piqué and into the far corner.

Harry strikes against Barcelona – yet another famous club on his list of victims.

TOTTENHAM HOTSPUR VS WOLVERHAMPTON WANDERERS
Premier League
29 December 2018

Harry loves a long, curling shot and this one was a classic. He had the ball at walking pace on the right a few yards outside the box. The defenders wanted to show him outside, but Harry had other ideas. He executed an audacious turn and headed infield, despite three tensed defenders waiting for him to enter the box. They were left watching as he bent a magnificent 20-yard fizzing shot into the far corner. Just brilliant.

It's his name on the scoresheet again, but Harry always recognizes the contribution of his team-mates and the fans.

MANCHESTER UNITED VS TOTTENHAM HOTSPUR
Premier League
27 August 2018

Harry's towering 50th-minute header sent Spurs on their way to a famous victory at Old Trafford. When Kieran Trippier's out-swinging corner cleared the near-post defenders, it was always going to be dangerous. Harry backed away from the penalty spot to gain space from marker Phil Jones and was still backing away when the ball reached him. No matter. With a colossal leap he arched his back and sent a 12-yard looping but powerful header back past goalkeeper David De Gea and into the net.

Harry's trademark air-punch celebration has become a familiar sight to Spurs fans.

BORUSSIA DORTMUND VS TOTTENHAM HOTSPUR
UEFA Champions League
5 March 2019

Dortmund tried desperately to come back from a 3–0 first leg defeat, but Harry's superb 47th-minute finish put the tie beyond reach. As Moussa Sissoko's slide-rule pass split the German defence, Kane, delaying his run to stay onside, picked the ball up 15 yards from the penalty area. One touch took the ball to the edge of the area and, looking up to see the oncoming keeper and a defender rushing to cover, Harry side-footed home with power and accuracy.

CHAMPIONS LEAGUE ADVENTURES

"Glory, Glory Nights" was the name given to the great European ties at the old White Hart Lane stadium. Now Harry Kane's performances in Spurs' all-white European strip have helped bring back a touch of glory in the 21st century.

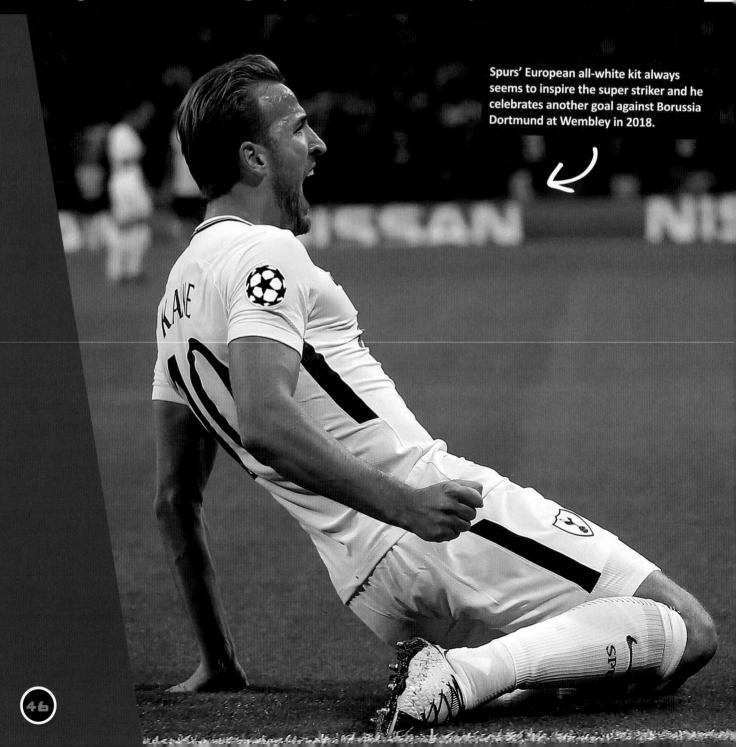

Spurs' European all-white kit always seems to inspire the super striker and he celebrates another goal against Borussia Dortmund at Wembley in 2018.

Back in 2017, Harry spoke of his desire to break into the "world-class bracket" by making his mark in the Champions League. He has certainly done that, becoming the fastest player to score nine goals in European Cup history doing it in his first nine games in the competition.

Harry struck in his last two games in the 2016–17 campaign, but it was the two goals at Wembley – a rampaging run and strike and a smart low drive – against Borussia Dortmund in the following season that showed he meant business. He stressed the point against Apoel Nicosia where a perfect left foot, right foot, header trio marked his first Champions League hat-trick. Although he didn't score in the famous 3-1 victory over Real Madrid at Wembley, he provided a great assist for Christian Eriksen's goal and, away to Juventus in the knockout stage, he coolly rounded keeper Gianluigi Buffon to earn Spurs a draw. At home, despite Harry hitting the inside of the post in the dying moments, Tottenham could not overcome the Italians.

Despite Harry scoring four in four games, Spurs initially struggled in the 2018–19 campaign in a group containing Inter Milan, PSV and Barcelona. Then fortunes changed. Needing a result in Spain, Harry was denied by a goal-line clearance, but set up Lucas Moura's late equalizer with a pin-point cross to send Spurs through. Harry missed the first leg of the knockout match against Borussia Dortmund, but returned for the away tie – clinching the win with a marvellously taken goal after being put clear by Moussa Sissoko.

What happened next is part of Tottenham Hotspur history as astonishing victories over Manchester City and Ajax took them to their first ever Champions League final. For Harry though it was bitter-sweet. He sustained an ankle injury after 56 minutes of the first leg of the quarter-final and missed those games and the rest of the league season. Somehow, by June, he was fit to face Liverpool in the final – the biggest game in the club's history. He played his part in a brave display, but was unable to help them recover from an unfortunate early penalty. He had to be content with a runners-up medal, but Harry had come closer than ever to glory.

Harry in action against Manchester City in the first-ever UEFA Champions League match at the new Tottenham Hotspur Stadium.

ON THE TRAINING GROUND

Harry Kane's success has been inspired by an American football star, aided by coaches and ex-players, and driven by his own obsessive desire to improve.

"I've probably had to work harder than most to get to where I am," Harry has admitted. He is blessed to have worked under great coaches at Tottenham Hotspur and in the England set-up, but so much of the credit has to go to the man himself for his willingness to learn and his dedication to improving as a footballer.

The man Harry cites as his inspiration plays a totally different sport: American football. In his early years at Spurs, Harry repeatedly watched a documentary on gridiron superstar Tom Brady. It recounted how the quarterback was overlooked as a young player, but succeeded through obsessive training and preparation.

The similarities in their stories hit home. Harry, already exceptionally hard-working in training, re-doubled his efforts. Former Spurs midfielder Sandro has recalled how some established players would mock the hard-working youngster saying, "The poor guy thinks he's going to get in the team!" but he worked on his positioning, stamina and strength, and stayed behind after training to work on his finishing.

Harry would also listen. Former England striker Les Ferdinand was a coach at Spurs who passed on invaluable advice; Mauricio Pochettino brought new ideas on improving fitness and speed; and, when Harry hit the

Gylfi Sigurðsson (now at Everton) was a role model and mentor for Harry as he strove to improve his game.

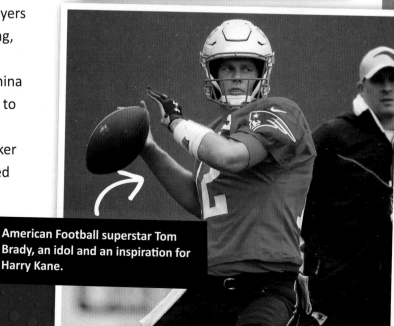

American Football superstar Tom Brady, an idol and an inspiration for Harry Kane.

inevitable goal drought, he took Alan Shearer's words on the need for self-belief to heart.

Harry has continued to work tirelessly on the training field and utilizes any marginal gains he can give himself. Pochettino revealed that Harry has a house near the training ground so he can be completely focused on his preparation; he works with sports scientists to improve areas such as sprinting; employs his own chef to ensure he eats properly; and, like his hero Brady, constantly re-watches matches, analyzing his own and other players' performances.

Harry's dedication to becoming the best continues to impress his coaches. Gareth Southgate called him a meticulous professional who sets the standard every day, while Pochettino has remarked that, "He is so determined, you need to stop him training, because he always wants to train, to improve – it is amazing!"

Harry at training with his Spurs' team-mates. His desire to keep improving has been noted by every coach he has played under.

THE UNASSUMING SUPERSTAR

Harry Kane's goalscoring exploits for Tottenham and England have made him a household name. Harry's focus is always on improving as a player, but celebrity has given him some interesting opportunities.

In December 2018, as Harry Kane was preparing for Tottenham's match against Southampton, he received an urgent call from his fiancée Katie. "She would never call me just before the match... I thought something was wrong!" he said afterwards. It turned out she was so excited because Harry had received a letter from the Queen saying he'd been awarded an MBE. Recognition in the New Year Honours list was a fitting accolade for the modest and likeable player who had done so much for club and country.

Harry is all about hard work and dedication. He is not the kind of player who is photographed leaving nightclubs in the early hours, he doesn't court publicity and, although he posts on Instagram and Twitter, he is always respectful and courteous. His advertising and sponsorship deals are also modest. He has an agreement to wear Nike boots and appeared in their advert celebrating London's diversity. He also has a partnership with the aptly named shaving brand Harry's and is key to their #IAmNotAfraid campaign, which highlights mental health issues.

Harry's profile was, of course, raised by his World Cup goalscoring feat. Cristiano Ronaldo even posted a picture on Instagram of himself and Harry Kane morphed into one, labelling it "Kanaldo"! Harry returned from Russia to find his image had been etched onto six five pound notes in commemoration of the number of goals he had scored in the finals, while Nike also marked Harry's achievement, presenting him with a pair of golden football boots bearing the legend "Lane, Lion, Leader".

Although he shuns the limelight, Harry has occasionally enjoyed the perks offered to celebrities. A big music fan, he walked the red

The MBE medal, received by Harry Kane at Buckingham Palace in March 2019 for services to football.

carpet and took to the stage with Camila Cabello at the Brits in 2018. In terms of dreams, he trumped that a year later when, taking advantage of being out injured, he flew to Atlanta to watch his beloved New England Patriots beat the Los Angeles Rams in Super Bowl LIII. He met his heroes Tom Brady and Julian Edelman and was even pictured with the winners' Vince Lombardi Trophy, but was soon back in training, desperate to help his club and country to trophies of their own.

Mutual admiration. Harry shares a hug with Cristiano Ronaldo after Tottenham played Real Madrid in 2017.

GREAT ENGLAND GOALS

Harry had started just 30 matches for the national side when he took his place among England's top 20 goalscorers. Among his 22 goals were some great individual strikes, crafted team moves and goals that were critical to the national team's fortunes.

ENGLAND VS GERMANY
International friendly
26 March 2016

England were 2–0 down when, with his back to goal, Harry picked up a cleared England corner at the edge of the area. No-one expected what followed. With a neat Cruyff turn Harry wrong-footed his marker, and fired a low shot through defender Emre Can's legs, across keeper Manuel Neuer's full-length dive and in off the inside of the post. The goal rocked the world champions and inspired England to a famous victory.

ENGLAND VS COLOMBIA
FIFA World Cup round-of-16
3 June 2018

At the end of extra-time in Moscow, Harry Kane could hardly run. But after Radamel Falcao had scored Colombia's opener in the shoot-out, there was no way the captain was going to shirk his duty. He had blasted his first two tournament penalties into the top left corner and earlier had coolly shot straight down the middle. Under such pressure, he took a few stuttering steps and drove the ball low and hard into the bottom corner. He really was Captain Cool.

Harry finishes a sensational solo goal in against Germany in 2016.

ENGLAND VS SCOTLAND
FIFA World Cup Qualifier
10 June 2017

In Harry Kane's first match as captain, two late Scottish goals looked to have derailed England's World Cup qualifying campaign, but Harry just couldn't let that happen. With perfect timing, he met Raheem Sterling's injury-time cross at the six-yard box on the far post. The finish was far from easy – he had to volley a knee-high ball coming across his body at pace – but, under incredible pressure, he dispatched it with great composure.

Harry broke Scottish hearts with his added-time equalizer at Hampden Park.

ENGLAND VS CROATIA
UEFA Nations League
18 Nov 2018

England were staring at relegation from the UEFA Nations League top tier when Ben Chilwell steadied himself to fire one last free-kick into the area. Everyone expected the near post defender to clear the low cross, but the ball fizzed past the lunge of the Croatian and across the six-yard box. There were four defenders waiting and just one man in white – Harry Kane. No prizes for guessing who was most alert in that split second, sliding to poke the ball in with his outstretched right foot. It was another vital late, late show from the captain and it sent England through to the semi-finals.

At full stretch, Harry nabs a priceless last-gasp winner against Croatia.

HARRY KANE RECORD-BREAKER

PREMIER LEAGUE

Only person to score against each of the 28 teams he has faced in the Premier League

Most Premier League goals in a calendar year – 39

Best strike-rate in Premier League history – 0.69 goals per game, a shade ahead of Sergio Aguero

Second-fastest to 100 Premier League goals – 141 games (Alan Shearer – 124 games)

Most Premier League hat-tricks in a year – 6 (2017)

Most goals scored on New Year's Day in the Premier League – 5 (record shared with Andrew Cole and Steven Gerrard)

One of only five players to have scored hat-tricks in consecutive league games (with Les Ferdinand, Ian Wright, Didier Drogba and Wayne Rooney)

Most Premier League Player of the Month awards – 6 (record shared with Steven Gerrard)

TOTTENHAM HOTSPUR

Tottenham's Premier League top goalscorer – 125 goals

Most Tottenham goals in a Premier League season – 30 goals in 2017–18

Tottenham's leading scorer in European competition – 24 goals

Tottenham's fourth all-time scorer in official competitions – 164 goals

First Tottenham player to score 20 goals in five straight seasons

Statistics as of 9 June 2019

ENGLAND

Appeared and scored at every youth level

Strike rate for first 20 goals – 0.59 goals per game (bettered only by Gary Lineker in modern times)

Scored the third-fastest England debut goal – 79 seconds

Set post-war record of scoring in six consecutive England appearances

Most goals by an England player in a single senior tournament – six (record shared with Gary Lineker, 1986)

Second England man to win World Cup Golden Boot

First hat-trick by an England captain at a World Cup

Scored in each of his first eight matches as captain

MISCELLANEOUS

Most goals at Wembley – 37 goals in 56 games

Most goals of any player in Premier League Tottenham v Arsenal North London derbies – 9

Europe's top goalscorer in 2017 – 56

Harry, currently Spurs' fourth leading goalscorer, has sights set on the great Jimmy Greaves's record of 266 goals.

Harry celebrates another goal in his already outstanding England career.

UEFA NATIONS LEAGUE HERO

As England captain, Harry led from the front in an ever more impressive Nations League campaign. Now as much a playmaker as goalscorer, he really was his country's talisman.

England had the perfect opportunity to follow up their World Cup success in the new UEFA Nations League. Harry was once again captain as England made an unlucky start with a harshly disallowed equalizer in a defeat to Spain. Then, in a 0–0 draw in Croatia, Harry's header crashed against the bar – consigning him to a six-match run without scoring for England.

If all the optimism of the summer was drifting away, it positively gushed back as England took a 3–0 first-half lead in Spain in October. Harry was chief orchestrator as his and England's pace destroyed the Spaniards. He failed to score as England held on to a famous 3–2 victory, but had a hand in every goal: a pin-point pass to Raheem Sterling, fantastic target-man play to set up Marcus Rashford and an pull back at full-stretch across goal for Sterling's second.

The Spanish press raved about England's striker. *Marca* wrote: "Kane is a 'Lord', so intelligent, a man who knows football outside the area too." *El País* said "Maybe it's the eyes, the sad face, but here's a silent genius ... He doesn't appear on the highlights reel, but did it all to bring Spain to their knees."

At Wembley England now faced Croatia in a match that could see them win the group or be relegated. Drawing 1–1 with five minutes to go, League B looked to be their destination, but Harry never gives up. Somehow he found room

in a crowded penalty area to get his boot on Ben Chillwell's cross. His first England goal for 747 minutes sent England to the finals in Portugal.

He found the scoresheet again at the start of the European Championship qualifiers in March 2019.

The captain leads the celebrations after Marcus Rashford's strike against Spain.

A penalty against the Czech Republic and a simple finish in a 5–1 demolition of Montenegro brought his tally to 22. However, by time the Nations League semi-final came around in June, Harry – again suffering from an ankle injury – had played just once in two months and that was just days earlier in the Champions League final.

Against the Netherlands, Gareth Southgate's young team again suffered disappointment as they lost in extra time, but they salvaged pride by winning the third place play-off against Switzerland. Harry showed glimpses of his old self, particularly with an audacious chip in the play-off that hit the crossbar, but there was no hiding his frustration at the way his season had ended.

Harry shows passion and pride as he celebrates his winner against Croatia.

AWARDS AND HONOURS

Harry has won the Premier League Player of the Month award on a joint-record six occasions.

World Cup Golden Boot winner 2018

UEFA Champions League runners-up 2018–19

FA Premier League runners-up 2016–17

Football League Cup runners-up 2014–15

FIFA World Cup Fan Dream Team 2018

Premier League Golden Boot winner 2015–16, 2016–17

England Player of the Year Award 2017, 2018

Tottenham Hotspur Player of the Year 2014–15

PFA Young Player of the Year 2014–15, **nominee** 2016–17

FA Premier League Player of the Month January 2015, February 2015, March 2016, February 2017, September 2017, December 2017

PFA Premier League Team of the Year 2014–15, 2015–16, 2016–17, 2017–18

PFA Fans' Player of the Year 2016–17

Football Supporters' Federation Player of the Year 2017

PFA Player of the Year nominee 2014–15, 2015–16, 2016–17, 2017–18

FWA Player of the Year runner-up, 2014–15

Awarded the MBE (Member of the Most Excellent Order of the British Empire), 28 December 2018

Millwall FC Young Player of the Season 2011–12

Harry and the England crowd celebrate his 2018 World Cup Golden Boot award.

"I'm very passionate about our country and very patriotic," said Harry on collecting his MBE.

59

WHAT'S NEXT FOR HARRY KANE?

Amazingly, at 26 years old, Harry Kane is yet to hit the peak years of a footballer. His ambition knows no bounds and trophies, records, even a career in American Football, are all on the wish list...

Harry has achieved so much in such a short time. He has helped establish Spurs as one of the top teams in the country and a force to be reckoned with in Europe; under his captaincy England reached a World Cup semi-final for the first time in his lifetime; and he has set goalscoring records for club and country. However, anyone who has followed Harry's career will know he will want to accomplish so much more in the future.

In June 2018 Harry signed a £10 million-a-year contract that commits him to Tottenham Hotspur until 2024. "People say this is maybe the best team we've had, maybe the best team we'll ever have – and the best manager," he told ESPN. "But it's important that we have something to show for it." If he helps win those elusive trophies, he could become the ultimate club legend. He is currently fourth in Spurs's all-time scorers chart, but needs around 100 more goals – four or five more seasons banging them in for Spurs – to overtake the great Jimmy Greaves at the top. It's possible.

For England, Harry has already tasted semi-finals in the World Cup and the Nations League. Can he take the team even further? London is hosting the Euro 2020 semis and final, and, with a young team coming of age together, prospects for the 2022 World Cup are good. Could we see Harry lifting the World Cup trophy in Qatar? By that time, he may

have become England's highest ever goal-scorer. Current leader Wayne Rooney has gone on record predicting Kane will break his 53-goal record.

Harry watches the Super Bowl in Atlanta in February 2019. It is his dream to play in the American Football showpiece.

Harry will be hoping to lead England to success in the World Cup in Qatar in 2022.

Harry's attitude to training and fitness should enable him to have a long career. Some speculate that he might leave Spurs for a richer English club or to play in Europe.

Harry, however, has hinted at only one career possibility: in 10 or 12 years' time he sees himself playing as an American Football kicker in the NFL. He's asked, "If you play in the Premier League and the World Cup, and you then play in the NFL, would you then be considered one of the greatest sportsmen ever?" The answer is undoubtedly, yes!

Harry celebrated Spurs' semi-final victory over Ajax with Dele Alli. Winning trophies for Tottenham Hotspur is still his number one ambition.

QUIZ

1 Against which team did Harry make his Premier League debut in August 2012?
a) Newcastle United **b)** Swansea City **c)** Fulham

2 Against which side did he score his first Premier League goal in a 5–1 win for Tottenham in 2014?
a) Chelsea **b)** West Ham United **c)** Sunderland

3 Against which country did he score his first goal for England on his debut in a Euro 2016 qualifier in 2015?
a) Lithuania **b)** Estonia **c)** Latvia

4 How many times has he been named Premier League Player of the Month?
a) Four **b)** Five **c)** Six

5 He is the second-fastest player in Premier League history to reach 100 goals behind Alan Shearer – how many games did it take him?
a) 132 **b)** 141 **c)** 150

6 How many times has he won the Premier League Golden Boot?
a) Twice **b)** Three times **c)** Four times

7 Which was the first club he was loaned out to?
a) Norwich **b)** Millwall **c)** Leyton Orient

8 With which sporting brand does he have a sponsorship deal?
a) Puma **b)** Under Armour **c)** Nike

9 What shirt number did he wear at the 2018 FIFA World Cup?
a) 9 **b)** 10 **c)** 11

10 What is the first name of his partner?
a) Sarah **b)** Katie **c)** Ellie

11 In what year does his current contract at Tottenham Hotspur expire?
a) 2020 **b)** 2022 **c)** 2024

12 Against which country did he score a hat-trick for England?
a) Panama **b)** Tunisia **c)** San Marino

13 How many times had he scored against Arsenal by the end of the 2018–19 season?
a) Seven **b)** Eight **c)** Nine

14 What is his middle name?
a) Edward **b)** James **c)** John

15 What number shirt has he not worn at Spurs?
a) 10 **b)** 23 **c)** 37

16 Which Premier League team has he not scored against?
a) Manchester City **b)** Stoke City **c)** None

17 What national honour did he receive in 2019?
a) CBE **b)** MBE **c)** OBE

18 How many goals did he score in the 2017 calendar year?
a) 30 **b)** 48 **c)** 56

19 How many managers has he played under at Tottenham Hotspur?
a) Two **b)** Three **c)** Four

20 Against which country did he first captain his country?
a) Lithuania **b)** France **c)** Scotland